Enlightened

by

Defilement

Some of the haiku and/or haibun in this collection previously appeared in the following journals: The Haibun Journal; Presence; Modern Haiku; Failed Haiku; Trillium Anthology of Haiku Canada; Haiku Canada Review.

Library and Archives Canada Cataloguing in Publication

Title: Enlightened by defilement : haibun : an almost memoir / by Vera Constantineau.
Other titles: Haibun : an almost memoir | Almost memoir
Names: Constantineau, Vera, 1951- author.
Identifiers: Canadiana (print) 20220456291 | Canadiana (ebook) 20220456321 |
ISBN 9781988989617
   (softcover) | ISBN 9781988989655 (EPUB)
Subjects: LCGFT: Haibun. | LCGFT: Autobiographical poetry. | LCGFT: Poetry.
Classification: LCC PS8605.O586 E55 2023 | DDC C811/.6—dc23

Printed and bound in Canada on 100% recycled paper.
Cover Artwork: Vera Constantineau
Cover Design: Chippy Joseph

Published by:
Latitude 46 Publishing
info@latitude46publishing.com
Latitude46publishing.com

We acknowledge the support of the Ontario Arts Council, Canada Council for the Arts, and the Ontario Media Development Corporation for their generous financial support.

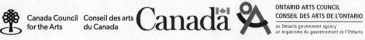

Enlightened by Defilement

Haibun: An Almost Memoir

Vera Constantineau

Ralph and Chloe
your constant support
means the world to me

Table of Contents

Introduction

Haibun is a centuries old Japanese literary form that envelopes both storytelling and poetry. These short prose pieces followed as they are by a relatable haiku satisfy both my poet side and prose side. In their creation haibun can include anything from travelogue to memoir, as is the case with Enlightened by Defilement. In their first-person structure each of my haibun tells you a bit about me, my life, and my experiences. The haiku is meant to give you a follow-up of sorts, a rest of the story ending. I have written honestly, from my memories which may be faulty, and from my family life. I hope when you finish reading through these pieces, you will know me better. None of us is without our secrets, I have not told you all of mine; secrets are ours to hold.

Introduction To Me

Number Eleven

I'm the firstborn child of Pat, but the eleventh child to live with Grace. Grace and Pat are mother and daughter. Pat gave me to Grace, who adopted me as her own. Now, I have a grandmother/mother and a mother/sister.

So begins the confusion that is my life. Five aunt/sisters and five uncle/brothers, half-sister/nieces and half-brother/nephews, not to mention the number of nephew-niece/cousins spawned by—well—you get it.

grade three
creating a family tree
tangled roots

MOM SAID

Keeping you was never the plan. You were here until your mom could take you. But time went on and decisions had to be made. We couldn't give you back, we'd got to like you. We had the children's aid lady to deal with, then the judge for the adoption procedure, and when you were eight, it was official. We were keeping you. We were never sorry.

hard questions
answered right
—maybe

The Day

We had to. Cancer, they said. A week they said. How could we have missed the signs? The weight loss we'd explained away because the appetite remained steady. Her playful spirit maintained. How were we to know? Twelve years in our lives. Not enough.

some would say
just a cat

Winter Nights

We sit near the wood burning parlour stove, each of us lost in our own thoughts. He reads the paper, or listens to the radio. If there's a funny bit, we laugh together. His hand is slow on the furry back, soothing the old Tom cat, warming him.

jealous
of the cat
on his lap

Her Garden

As soon as frost released the soil in her garden, she'd be outside. Down on her hands and knees she'd clear winter residue, loosen the fertile ground—patting the wet soil in the places she knew perennials were waiting to sprout. All of this care came after she'd raked the grass, pruned the hedge and mulched the shrubs. This morning the new owners tore out the hedge, ripped away the shrubbery, and flattened the flowering gardens. More parking they say, more parking.

sidewalk cracks safest path for ants

NONE OF THIS MATTERS TO ME—I'M RETIRED

Resting better now. No morning sleep broken by alarm clocks. No more fair-trading sweat to keep the wolf from the front and back doors. No more worrying about opening or locking up.

Rules like, "Don't sleep with the boss," no longer apply.

break time
scent of coffee
anytime

Risk And Reward

Thirteen. A popular age for folly. It's when I tried vice too. For my brother, it was a hook that set. For him it was a moment of silence, something to do with his hands. For him, the urge to quit came with the diagnosis. Too late.

the flick
of his lighter
last time

CHURCH OR BAR

In this small town the lines are firmly drawn between the drinkers and the abstainers. This is my experience. In our family it wasn't even church or bar. There was bootlegger in the dry days and when the liquor flowed freely, there was house party after house party. Church never really came up unless one of the religious types showed up at our door and tried to draw my mother into their fold, to which she'd always reply, "I've got my own church." The door would then be firmly shut.

doodle pad
changing the steeple
to a party hat

When I Was A Kid

When I was a kid the neighbourhood Grandma found the neighbourhood Grandpa, face down in the drive—snow shovel still in hand. When that happened, he was younger than I am now. I set my shovel back on the porch—boy next door—like a grandkid to me—he's always looking to make a buck—doesn't need that kind of memory of me.

pocketful of coins
jingling all the way
to spring

Around The Bend

I've followed the S-curve of the road, and find a field of perfectly ripened grain laying golden in the evening light washed with a hint of pink from the sunset. The stems swaying and swirling a wind dance that hurries away across the field and out of sight.

Today I've returned, driving with intention. My friend knows a surprise is in store. I shut off the motor and gesture grandly to the field, even more gloriously golden in the sun high overhead. The wind is still playing the stems and I wait for her reaction.

She doesn't see the colour or the beauty. What this former farmer's daughter saw was the hard work that lie ahead.

in dreams
snow-capped mountains
closer

New Start

Labour Day weekend and I'm in the back seat staring out the car window. Not that I can see much, it's dark. We've left the island I grew up on and are entering the city I will now call home. We're miles out, but I'm filled with anticipation. I'm going to a post-secondary school to take commercial courses that will set me up for my future.

the wind
a scent
of smelter chimney

I'm dropped off at the house where I have a room in the basement. I use my key to go inside. The homesickness kicks in immediately. That night I keep my transistor radio under my pillow turned on for company. New pillow, new bed, new clothes, I barely sleep.

invading ants
swarm a new hill

Soon I know my way to the home room. Soon I know where I can get a good meal for three dollars. Soon I find a friend and we bond over cheap dinners.

home for Christmas
twenty kilos heavier
a light heart

Go Home Road

That's what the sign reads ***Go Home Road.*** After seven decades of passing it, still, the urge to turn around is strong. The need to see my mother, check in on the old haunts, fills me. I have to keep a grip on the wheel. Go. Home. A wave of loss and guilt, the weight of responsibilities not met kicks me hard, the air in my lungs isn't enough, the tears in my eyes, unexpected.

missed exits
the roads ahead
unmarked

Two Across One Down

```
                L
C O N S T A N T I N E A U
                T
                T
      R E G R E T S
                R
                S
```

lost in fog
your name
on the gravestone

The Talk Of The Town

We got our first television when I was eight years old, black and white and second hand, with a quirky twitch that caused the picture to flip every few seconds. We got used to its habits as we developed our own. My mother, my sister and I were enthralled by the programs showing us places we'd read about but had never seen. There in our living room, we witnessed the Beatles' arrival to America and had an invitation into the Camelot world of the Kennedys but the best part was gathering for the gossip around the affairs in *Peyton Place*.

every night
an education
flipping out

The National News With Earl

Cuban missile crisis, but I'm barely aware. Earl Cameron is on the eleven o'clock broadcast giving more information than I can take in. My mother is afraid, so I am afraid too. We're watching the black and white, second-hand tv. Much-admired John F Kennedy has done something-something and the Russians are involved. There's a mention of pigs in a bay and then Earl's serious signoff to a commercial. My mother, in a rare move, puts her hand on my shoulder.

all the ways
the world has changed
and hasn't

And It Did

Large and black. Crow. It flew from a nearby tree to land on his shoulder. It turned one bright eye, then the other, seeking reassurance that here was a safe place. That on this flannel shirt, warm in the afternoon sun, it was welcome. No one expected panic to ensue, but it did.

old wives' tales
touching the cold
folded hands

The Phone Call After The Party

The approach is direct. The look exchanged is deep. The kiss, deeper.

You'd have laughed, I said. Then she said maybe, maybe not. I don't think adultery is funny. In response I said, but imagine the way they'd tucked themselves into the tight space between the refrigerator and the counter, as if it were the cool place, the invisible place. I laughed as I recalled the moment when I realized they were there and said, anyone could have walked in. She said, well, anyone, you, did walk in and what did they do. Nothing, I said, they did notice me so I wheeled around and got out of there.

best before
dates back in the day
filled with intrigue

Shifting Sand

I never wanted a house, but if I must have a house then it should be a nice one—spacious and well built in a good neighbourhood. It should have fashionable furnishings and an abundance of green plant life throughout. The kitchen should be sizable and of course, several bathrooms, if I must have a house.

casino outing
the woman next to me
hits the jackpot

CRAVING SILENCE

The silence I craved for so long arrived, bringing along companions, grief, loneliness and loss. Who could imagine silence so loud? Perhaps I could buy a ticking clock or rescue a barking dog. But then, it would be rude to treat my invited guest so. The wish was mine, yet if I could, I would go back in time and wish otherwise.

dark of the moon
a hint of his aftershave
prickles my nose

Radio Dreams

My sister and I lay facing each other on a sagging mattress. We're listening to DJ Bobby O on Z103.3—the volume turned low. It's four a.m., the night air sizzles. We anticipate the coming storm.

    Don't touch, Bobby growls, *don't touch that dial.*

We've kicked the sheet to the foot of the bed. His voice sinks into us as we lay in our underwear. We imagine he's speaking to us, his deep voice offering a *ménage à trois.*

Mom and dad are asleep, oblivious in their room down the hall.

    Step in, step into my audio parlour—be one with me.

We smile at the familiar invitation. Bobby is our middle of the night bad girl rebellion. He's the man in our lives who whispers things just before we sleep. He incites dreams we never share, hopes we can't yet voice.

    Let my champagne and caviar late night ramble lift you from the bog of your mundane lives.

His words entice. Champagne. Caviar. We imagine escaping our small-town lives to meet him in some seductive setting.

    Feel your cares slide away, nothing noxious here my lovelies.

We shift, made restless by his words. Feel? What do we feel?

    Just gentle words and soft songs. That's what I'm delivering, it's love baby, love.

Then, the crackle of lightning; the ripple of thunder

small town
only the streetlights
are upstanding

Player

Love him. I play his music over and over. Everyone in the house is sick of the sound of his voice, but not me. I fall asleep whispering his name. My ticket is a talisman I touch every night before drifting into dreams.

Tonight, the smell of bodies, the tingle of excitement surrounds me. The band kicks it up, I close my eyes and there is the voice that has vibrated inside me. It reaches out to me. When the song ends, I open my eyes.

The realization is crushing. He's mortal. Just a man. Smaller than in my dreams. Again, he leans into a song, but for me it's over. Loneliness returns on a guitar riff. I'm back to *dancing in the dark*—alone.

night bird
a sheen of sweat
on my thighs

To Disappear

Now that I live in the city, I'm just one more moving object on the sidewalk. I wanted that. To be anonymous. To withdraw erotica from the library. To explore other lifestyles. To eat hot foods and drink exotic drinks. I have that now. Laughing loudly earns me no strange looks. In this city, freedom isn't a myth.

amber alert
midnight stranger
in town

Meanings Of Life

The house on the overgrown corner lot across from ours lies abandoned. No glass in the windows. No doors. Only morning glories thrive. Against the frame of the second storey window a rotting ladder leans precariously. This gives me no joy. I too am in a house with no escape.

I pour his second cup of tea. The baby cries. I'm reminded that I am needed.

morning glories
nowhere to go
but up

Lemons

Another cold month has come with a cotillion of snow-dressed clouds. Trees bow and even their naked shadows are touched with white lace. I long for seasons where snow does not block the door. Seasons where I have no need for coat or gloves. I long for the days when sunlight rolls across the floor like an open bag of lemons, bright and almost blinding with the glare. How happy I will be, to watch ice melt away in a jug of lemonade.

dresses
in the cedar cupboard
abandoned

Inside Voices

The air in the kitchen is heavy with the scent of garlic and basil. The family-recipe lasagna will be perfect, how can it not? I hurry to shower and change into the yellow top and red capri pants picked out earlier in the day. My husband asks if he should wear a tie and I laugh, but that he'd given the evening the weight it deserves is obvious. We can do nothing to alter what's done. The ring is on the finger. Vows have been taken. The die is cast. I hear voices and hurry up the hallway. Still out of sight, I hear our new son-in-law speak for the first time. "Oh no...not garlic, he says"

the taste for love
doled out in small portions
forgiveness

Care In The World

The stay in hospital goes on for weeks. I miss my family, my own bed. Still, I miss walking without pain more. The surgeon assures me I am going to be much better after a hip replacement. My husband visits on the weekend bringing my handicap scooter. We slip into the fall sunshine and, in our enthusiasm, the tour grows too long, the battery dies. He leaves me near a corner garage to retrieve our van from the hospital parking lot.

Hospital stays create no beauty queens, I look awful. Weight loss. Messy hair. Ugly jogging suit. Add in the battery fail near a dumpster where several garbage bags are lined up. I realize I look homeless with goods piled close. No one passing is making eye contact. I'm feeling less and less happy. A paper bag falls out of the air near me. I'm startled. Then fearful.

across the street
a homeless man shouts
you eat it then

The Idealists Worn To Dust

I am drawn to news of the election, now only days away. On the
tv screen, I watch as a fistful of gravel comes at the candidate from
behind. The arena parking lot erupts in shouts and jeers. Childhood
warnings rush in—don't throw rocks.

feinting left
with full awareness
behind the smile

Making A Difference With His Dollars

The year the Conservative Party of Canada claims power for the first time, our shuffling old neighbour, Oscar, brings Dixie Cup ice cream sundaes to the house. Strawberry for him and mom, butterscotch for my sister and me.

Oscar and Mom are cautiously optimistic. "Let's wait and see," they say. Then slip the wooden spoon over their toothless gums.

field of wild roses another party in the house

Introduction To Science

I'm five and I have inherited a box of rejected treasures, including a wind-up clock. My brother, always in the market for a deal, offers me a dime for the timepiece. I accept.

I head to the store for a small bag of candy. When the candy bag is empty, I go back inside.

There, on the table, sits his clock beside a basin of water which my mother, interrupted by a call, is using to wipe down shelves. The question . . . will a clock tick under water, comes to me from nowhere. Question, meet Opportunity. The answer is no. Once a clock has been submerged the ticking will stop.

When my brother gets home, he finds his clock on the table, somewhat heavier, being water logged as it is. He wants his dime back

clockface
caught in a sunbeam
idle hands

Learning Curve

A six-year-old and a seven-year-old are left alone in a front yard where the push lawn mower with its sharp shiny rotary blade has also been left carelessly abandoned. We're drawn to it, my best friend and I. We discuss what to do and agree that we're going to experiment. We'll chop a leaf. She chooses to hold the leaf and I will push the mower.

wedding day
the tip of her ring finger
still missing

Thereafter Every Sunday For Months

In spring northern moods grow lighter as the sun shines longer into the evening. One night my mother, a traditional cook, surprised us with a walk on the wild side. She hums as she fits a fair-sized stick of wood in the cookstove. Out comes a flashy yellow box with red lettering. She holds it aloft and announces, "We're having peecha." Skipping the directions, she kneads and prebakes the crust brown before smearing on a thin layer of the deep red sauce. She sprinkles the powdered cheese on top and bakes the pizza another twenty minutes. The crust's edge has to be chipped loose of the pan, but the new taste is a hit. Every Sunday for months we silently gnaw our way through this treat.

in a box
on the windowsill
fresh herbs

GINGER AND BEER: NEVER IN THE SAME SENTENCE

My mother doesn't know what we do when my new friend and
I hang out together. We've biked way past the town line. We've
eaten a packet of salted-top soda biscuits from a tin her mother
keeps in the cupboard. We've sneaked a ginger beer from her
basement and shared it. None of this is allowed at my house. There
are rules about bike riding and at home the crackers are for soup.
One day, early spring, we headed downtown. I'm supposed to be
at my friend's house, but we decided to explore the big ditch near
the main road. Snow melted left rapidly rushing water. From the
edge I stepped out onto a rock that's not a rock. A log shifts and I
tumbled in. It was freezing, I began to sink. She grabbed my coat
and hauled me up. Another close call.

new rules
homework first
before frolic

THE STEAL

Saturday. My friends and I are inside the summer kitchen at their house. The place is a mess, every surface is piled with jars, pails, and newspapers among other, some smelly, things. We've got plans to steal apples from the bushel-basket their father brought home. We're quiet, not easy when there are five of us. We send one of the youngest to the toilet to create a cover. Their mother is a scant ten feet away, behind the half-open door. Experience has taught us she can hear a fly breathe. And then she's shouting at us. As long as we're out of arms reach, we don't fear her, it's all shout. We fill our hands and we run to our hideout to eat our fill.

sound of heartbeats
loud in our ears

On A Bright And Sunny Day

My brother climbs to the highest possible branch, which is forbidden. Hanging upside down high in the solid branches like a monkey, or maybe a sloth, slowly taking everything in. Mother frets as he reports on the condition of the roof, the color of the last car in line to cross the ancient swing bridge leaving our island, and he tells her Aunt Ethel is on her way to visit. As much as she begs, he will not come down. Not until bedtime does he return to solid ground.

first a hug
then a swat
love's order

First Kiss

Fall evening, full moon over his shoulder. My thoughts line up like cars in the pack at a Nascar race, each clamoring for space. He leans in, his face shadowed now. His lips press mine, his eyes close, the moon still shining in the night sky. As a reader of romance novels, I believed there would be fireworks, explosions, but there's just his warmth, his scent, and the knowledge that fiction, even if romantic, is still fiction. Years later, a new moon, warm kisses, anniversary cards and vows kept.

time passes
in a breath
between us

On The Rocks

I'm little, not even in school yet and neither is my best friend. We're on the shale rock pile looking for the perfect size of shards to use as play money. We gather, we rise, head toward the haw trees. Running on the loose shale is like running on water. I go down hard. I shriek. My sister comes at a trot. She's bigger, older and comforting. My knee is sliced open. Against the deep tan, the white tissue is stark in contrast. I begin to cry. Bone. I'm convinced the white matter is bone. There's no blood, yet. My sister picks me up and lugs me home to mother. No stitches. No hug. Only recriminations.

kneecap hits table leg
falling through time
childhood pain

SOFT SHOULDERS ROUNDED ARMS AND JIGGLY BUMS

The three of them, Grace, Edna and Eunice, would gather at Edna's place. I'd be given a colouring book and crayons and ignored for the most part while they gossiped and giggled as three sisters do. When the evening wore on enough, mom and Eunice would start making noises about heading home, and Edna would always say *I'll walk part way with you.* Up the dirt road they'd go with me dragging along behind.

At the crossroads where mom and I would turn left toward home and Aunt Eunice would turn right, they'd laugh and one of them would bump a fleshy hip against the other, making fun because Edna was still with them. Night after summer night, Eunice would say the same words, *come to my place, we'll have a lunch.* Off we would go to feast on sliced canned ham on white bread or crackers with butter and pickles.

she died
while I was away
scent of lavender

Sobering

Drunk anger. Fierce ugly words. Mean eyes. Quick hands. Near death scare. Sobering. Relief.

Love. No trust. Years without. Jealousy arises. Ugly. Angry. Slip. Quickly drunk. Wrapped in fear. Shred of sense. Sober.

all the steps
one day another day
break new ground

A Shadow's Life Is Real

Some will say it's not for me to judge, but didn't I witness tears, listen to a heart's yearnings,watch conjured hope fade when no promise was real, so I say, you go ahead, boy. Put on the dress-up suit, march your clicking heels to the edge of the edge and jump in.

bleeding hearts
bounce on their vine
sowing bad seed

This Is Where We Are Now, The Plum Tree And Me

I've sat in on your fallow period, smelled beginnings on the sweetest wind. The interim, where work is done, where all that lies ahead rests in hope and dogma, stretches onward. Then the plums, fewer than the blossoms promised, but such is the way with time.

grandchildren
nearby and scattered
the deepest roots

Change

The water of the north channel with its ebb and flow follows the direction of the wind—with confidence meeting uncertainty it will return. A wave rises, not at my feet, but in my core, anticipation for a life to come while running from the life I've been given. Grow up. Find happiness. Find self.

lists grow
suitcase remains the same
for years

Places To Go

The day I graduate from grade eight my older brother gives me a bicycle. I know how to ride one, I've used my neighbour's for years. It's too big for me, and I've had a few incidents, but nothing that wasn't my own fault. Like the time I tried to ride it with no hands while standing on the pedals. I can still feel the burn as I admire my own new wheels. This one is a little too big for me too, and it has an oddly high crossbar design feature. I get on and my brother adjusts the seat as far down as it will go. He adjusts the handlebars and the pedals as much as he can. I get on to give it a try and my mother's worst fear comes home to roost. I am free. As I move off down the drive, she says to my brother, "She'll never be home now."

growing up
on those untraveled roads
wind at my back

Years on, my mother is visiting me in the city. On Saturday, we catch the bus and head over to the car dealership a few miles away. We walk up and down the rows of used cars. No one approaches us. The place is closed, says so on the sign in the big front window. We wait at the bus shelter and when the bus wheezes to a stop we get on and go back to my place. I cook her dinner, using the recipe she recites to me.

soup in the pot
smelling like home
new place

A week later, my brother picks me up, takes me to a car lot where I buy my first car. He adjusts the seat and the steering wheel, pulls the mirror down so I can see. I wonder if he too hears the echo of our mother's voice saying, "She'll never be home now."

together
wearing out the tires
on familiar roads

Cooking With Scratch

My grandmother and my mother were good cooks. One was the basics: meat, potatoes and dessert. The other was foreign fare with a flair. My daughter wanders in toting laundry.

millennials
only on the move
never truly gone

As my grandmother did, and as my mother did for me, I've written every favourite recipe into a cookbook. My daughter's request— although I've shown her the recipes for most, right there, on the boxes. I fantasize about coq au Vin with pearl onions, tortiere with a flaky crust, rich browned gravy over a roast.

Next trip through the kitchen, before I've begun to cook, my daughter asks if we can order a pizza. I pull out my cookbook and choose the right take-out menu.

role models
not always teaching
the expected

In Less Than Sixty Seconds

No lady gets in a bar fight—ends up in a tipped over chair in a
sitting position thin back the only thing between her and the
floor where the stale smell of spilled beer, cigarette smoke and
adultery lives—nobody will believe this would happen to a four-
foot something woman of no strength, yet here I am—skinny
arms wrapping over face warding off the other woman's clawing
red nails as she tries to gouge my eyes.

the bartender
who waters the drinks
saves me

Fantasy

He's alone at home in front of the LED fireplace, sipping sparkling juice from a champagne flute, eating carob treats close at hand on a small plastic dish lined with a lust-red paper napkin while she is home alone yearning for him

Valentine's day
litre of ice cream
cooling my heels

The Tall Red Apartment Building

It's a stopgap on the way to our new home. Again, the elevator. The doors glide open and the artist from two floors down, a lot of cachet, a newsworthy figure, steps in. I nudge my husband; we share a smile behind the celebrity's back. I tell my brother about these chance encounters and he says, "So? He used to paint lunch pails in the break room at the smelter. Next time you see him in the elevator, tell him Smitty says hello."

one shaft
another shaft
eye of the beholder

The Last Little One Sprays Spittle On Santa's Beard

I'm the hurried and harried, cartoon-stereotype, Christmas shopper.
I've rushed the gift search with no time to spare. I'm catching up
with friends. I walk out of a store gripping several bulging bags that
bang against my thighs and I'm swamped by a tired looking mom
and dad, three trudging boys, and in mama's arms a tiny little girl
just past wobbly with huge dark eyes and a tuft of dark hair. She
looks into my eyes—a heartbeat—she purses her lips and blows
a spectacular long, juicy, air-filled raspberry buzz of happiness.
There's mass confusion, what with three boys, two parents, my
shopping bags, and a raspberry blowing baby. We sort ourselves
out. I, serendipitously, turn the same way they do, and follow them
through the crowd. She blows raspberries all the way to Santa's lap.
I stop to watch, and I can't stop smiling.

under bar lights
every package
lit up

Every Practice Run Perfect

My sister and I arrive home. She's in charge of me since our mom is away. She unlocks and pushes the door open to a house full of smoke. My sister shrieks, "The house is on fire!" I never doubt anything she says so I bolt for my friend's house across the road where a fire phone is installed, as there are in every volunteer fireman's home. I burst through the door. Their grandma listens to my panicked words, catches "house on fire" and picks up the red fire phone to ask for help. I'm shaking with fear when Grandma wraps her soft full arms around me, pulls me against the front of her bibbed apron to sooth my cries and dry my tears. Big Red, the town fire truck, moans to a stop in front of our house. Men jump to the ground and rush through the door. Minutes later they come back out. Our supper, sitting on the oven rack is now nothing but ash.

the grapevine hanging heavy with new fruit

The Long And Crooked Path To Patience

I've cursed these arthritic fingers bent so as to never grasp what I long to grasp. In the yard, as is my habit, I watch my step. I look at the blades of green grass, note the jump-ups and clover that grow there. I see it, can't believe I see it, want to pick it, but cannot. So, I wait. I wait for someone to come outside. Someone I can call to me, to pick this first four-leaf clover I have found in my long life. A young woman, half my age, appears. I call to her and guide her verbally to the stem I want. She sees it. Her eyes brighten. She carefully tugs it free of the hundred other plain Jane clovers. She says she's been looking for one of these her whole life. Me too.

contorta
the twisted limbs
of a hazel

The Need To Leave

The summer races on. Day job. Friday night dances. The dream is getting away from all I know to move into the place where I know me and no one else. Most evenings I spend hours looking at the ancient swing bridge that connects the island to the mainland, and feel my heart beat.

leaving
the bus fills
with memories

My room is small, the walls covered with dark brown paneling. No sun comes in the window high on the basement wall. My only light is a flickering fluorescent tube hidden by a plastic shield. It vibrates.

the pillowcase
doesn't smell
like mom's

The school is huge and every day for a week I get lost. Lunch is the best part of my day next to supper. I have no friends.

a stranger
this shadow
that is me

Fall races on. I make a friend. We eat at a small restaurant nightly. Christmas, I return to my mother, familiar faces, and real food.

the pillowcase
doesn't smell
like mine

Back on the bus, this time filled with anticipation. My room, with
its new lamp, is no longer dim. A teacup my mother gave me is
in pride of place.

a nesting bird
in the window well
weaving a life

After graduation I pack up this life I've gathered and board the
bus. Across the bridge and up the hill for a visit.

THE AT HOME ATTITUDE DISAPPEARS

Mom curls and combs out her hair, gets dressed up and puts on her special shoes. Teeth, kept in a cup in the kitchen cupboard, are slipped into place. It's a drastic change. She's beautiful. I watch her speak, admiring her teeth. They're made of white porcelain formed with a small gap between the two front ones, just like the gap in mine.

unchanged
the smile I recall
in the mirror

The Affirmation Of The Inner Woman

The drawer is filled with lace and memories. The scent of lavender sachet meets nose. Choosing garments no one will see to wear under garments everyone will see, this takes time. A flash of red, a touch of black, a cup of this, a cup of that. Few will know what lies beneath.

rose petals
holding the scent
of a memory

Was The Heat Took Us

It was a Sunday and Grandma and I had the bay to ourselves

Delivered in a tone of wry humour

Let us go in, Grace, we'll be refreshed Grandma said.

They stripped to their petticoats, my grandma and my mother, wading into the sun-dappled Georgian Bay.

We walked until we were up to our ribs floating and laughing like girls as the white froth of cotton and lace rose to the surface belling out, like clouds around us. And that's when we heard the motor.

They ducked down, their bottoms close to bottom, their heads above the sunny surface. Hoping they wouldn't be spotted.

Hello, Mrs. Smiths a pair of fishermen called out on a wave. On your way, Grandma had shouted. And because she was commanding that way, they put-putted slowly around the bend and we hurried out and into our dresses.

in my voice mother's words

BRIDGES

The Funeral is over. We've taken off the suits and somber dresses. We're lounging in jeans and tees under a full sun. Lawn chairs in a family circle on the back yard grass, recovering from an overload of sorrow. Mother begins to tell a story. *It was a hard winter, and we were looking to spring. Sick to death of fish, fish and more fish the venison stew made a welcome change. The game warden picked that day to check in. He left late, coming on dusk, never said a word about the out of season deer meat. Mind, he'd eaten his fill too.*

first laugh after tears falling into silence

Because A Stroke Robbed Her Of Speech

She cannot rise
She cannot ask
She cannot comb
She cannot wash
She cannot lift a fork
She cannot eat
She cannot swallow
She cannot laugh
She cannot tell stories
She cannot sing
She cannot comfort
She cannot

hospital stay
every day
the same cloud

THE GRAY YARD

Gathered around, as always, those they'd known their whole lives.
Mrs. Bob and Bob with their children here and there across the
hill. The Smiths, the Lockyers, the bootlegger, the ne'er do wells,
the worthy. Names on headstones still clearly etched in enduring
granite and marble seeming out of place on this limestone island.
In the distance the La Cloche mountains rise like a Group of Seven
painting. Shades of somber muted evergreens and wind-play on
water.

the blue of her eyes a break in the clouds

HIS FINAL WORDS AT SEVENTY-THREE

His hand stroked the pale green hospital blanket, as if in his last dream he was petting Old Tom, his favourite cat. When he spoke, he was a boy again. His smile guileless, eyes wide and open. We listened to him breathe in and out. "I'll be a good boy, he said, I'll be a good boy." On his last breath

lights dimming
the sound of bells
and a raven's wing

HIT ME HE SAYS HIT ME

At thirteen years old, he was already an alcoholic—it was all
downhill after that.

broken promises
always at the bottom
of the first glass

Cup And Saucer Trail

It's not famous, but it is beautiful and close to home. Challenging in places because there are only rock handholds. In a few places my brother, taller and stronger, boosts me up. We reach the summit after an hour and a half of hiking. This is the day I realize I am afraid of heights. My brother seems to be unafraid of anything. He approaches the edge, laying down on his stomach, moves himself forward so he can spit over the edge.

Alzheimer's ward
he remembers none
of his escapades

The Neighbour Next Door

Issues. You know. When the moon is full there's a tendency for him to turn full wolf. Daylight, he is usually more human, but this morning the screen door took a wild ride off his balcony. I'm just grateful that it was the door and not the guy.

lines drawn
by the tide
full sail

Lonely Afternoons

There's a chill in the breeze through the open window as I sign my weekly letter to my brother. I've been told he's busy; that there's much for him to do. His regular barber's appointments, afternoon walks to the gazebo on the fringe of the property, walks to the mailbox and any other place he takes it into his head to go. And of course, there are the new people he meets every day. I place a stamp squarely in the corner of the envelope and seal the flap. Eighteen letters now. Sometimes I include a photograph or a poem he's always loved. What does he think when these letters with their tokens arrive, now that he's lost to Alzheimer's.

fenced in
watching traffic
on a nameless road

Nanny Goat

Today, the urge to call my brother, long gone and thus unreachable in the hereafter, overcame me. Say I could call. Say he could answer, I know we'd laugh over how our older brother, Nanny, would wear long underwear in the summer.

Nanny earned his nickname by being Nanny's *good boy.* Also, so-named for his tendency to head butt her legs for attention. The name stuck in his adult years due to his beeing "stubborn as a goat."

a recipe
irredeemable
once altered

My Brother

The down-the-block confirmed bachelor shy guy with the big heart
comes for dinner three times a week because we're both single
both have to eat we share the cost so why not and when dinner is
over we choose our favorite armchairs in the living room to talk
or watch tv then he gets up to head home he hates the carpet and
when our evening ends every time every time he walks out of the
living room backwards swiping his stocking feet from side to side
erasing his footprints from the nap replacing them with semi circles
of undetermined origin

after a storm
the clean sweep
of petals

CAN YOU IMAGINE

It never occurred to me to open the envelope with my name on the front set on the buffet in the front room. Mail was a serious thing in our house. Letters from my fourth oldest sister who lived out west were saved until after supper and read aloud to everyone. What we would have done if there'd been personal information meant for one person's eyes only, I learned when my third oldest sister found herself pregnant at a point when everyone assumed she was past that kind of shenanigans. That tidbit was read out one sentence before the line that said, "please keep this quiet for now."

When we'd settled down for the evening Mom handed out the envelopes. In turn, we popped the flaps. A thank you for attending the wedding, another thank-you for the gift I'd no idea I'd even given them. My sister looked equally mystified. I read on, "You looked like an angel in your new dress," my brother had written. I was floored. Our relationship was rocky. He was on record saying I'd been a thorn in his side forever. At five, I'd drowned his new alarm clock. At seven, I drew all over his bedroom wall. At ten, he took me hunting and set me off to walk down the train tracks. He walked parallel, out of sight, in the bush. It felt like a long time, I got worried after a while that he might be lost. I started yelling. He came out, breathing fire. He'd been on the trail of a rabbit. He said I scared it off, along with anything else he might have wanted to shoot.

"You looked like an angel in your new dress." The word angel was a new one from him. I believed him. After all, his name was scrawled at the bottom of the short message along with his new wife's. He'd signed it, love. Love.

a lifetime
of misunderstandings
late brother

For The First Time In My Life

Home to my mother is where I go. I am in need of comfort. Today we sit in her living room. I am on the sofa and she is tucked in the corner of the loveseat. I say, "I don't know how to go on." She says, "It isn't your choice to make." In that moment I realize she has misunderstood and thinks I want to kill myself. I aim for reassurance, but later, as she walks me out to my car, I realize something else. I have frightened her.

one hug
on the day I need it
one hug

My Mistake

Was assuming my birth mother and the man who would be my
stepdad, got married when I was thirteen days old. The truth, that
it was a year and thirteen days after, meant my half-brother, born
a year later and only nine days after their marriage was almost as
illegitimate as me.

unlucky number
one year, one moon
one son

His Dad Is Not My Dad My Dad Is A Cloud

His dad remembered my birthday, gave chocolates on Valentine's Day, taught me about hanging a stocking at Christmas, and fairness and equality, his dad taught me that.

art class
the careful outline
of a ghost

Unknown Relatives—Life Changing

The seasons are shorter in the place she lives, I know the growing season starts in July. We share a screwed-up woman and the man who is our grandfather. That woman is gone, he is too, and the truth is, we're not sad.

The thump of the airplane's wheels touching down sets my heart beating quicker. Her picture

has been in my mind for a long time. I know her, but still, will her skin smell like family? Will mine?

lavender sachet
she says there was a sale
I say—I know

My Dear,

years since we spoke
still—this yearning
lost sister

Today, I'm sorry. Years of wondering why you gave up on me
without a word, I get it. It was me.

I inserted myself into your life, hammered out walls, built on, not
realizing you were content

with who you were when you were alone. Then, the unforgivable, I
made your mom mine. I called when you didn't, showed up when
you couldn't, and that was it. I became the wedge I created.

Nothing can put back time that's lost. No one can take your place.
I lost, but perhaps you lost too. I did love you. In the future if I'm
against another wall, I hope my memory will stop me, remind me
that walls dissolve, and I will remember to stand alone.

tai chi
any resistance
imagined

Another Ride Around The Planets

She romps into the bedroom, all legs and arms, all bright eyes and smiles. She tells of seeing Neptune and Saturn through the lens of a friend's telescope. I make the proper noises, perhaps overly impressed that in the years since grade three science this budding social butterfly has taken an interest in the universe. As she is leaving, the door almost closed, I call out "But not Uranus, right?"

muffled laughter
valuable teaching tools
mother and child

Wasting Time—A Book's Cover Not The Story

On an early spring day, we're standing in the driveway of a house we're going to view. It's perfect. The price is right, the roof line and the surrounding shrubbery—a soon-to-bloom mauve lilac, tiny pink caragana buds and blossoms releasing their perfume, give the place a cozy cottage feel. We're waiting for the real estate agent to arrive with the key. I've a good feeling about this one, I turn to my husband and say, "We're going to be the Constantineaus of Evans Road." The agent arrives and is rather less than enthusiastic in his haste, so unlike the other times we've met. Bad news, there's a solid offer on the house and it's as good as sold. He gives us a tour anyway, so we can see what we've missed out on. I don't remember the interior afterward.

Months later, in early fall, we drive down Evans Road again, some kind of self-torture, a reflection of what might have been. Half way down the block we see a two-storey house with mustard-coloured siding and brown trim. Its roof is barn shaped, the yard is decent, there's a huge rickety garage. On the front step there's a cardboard box upon which someone has scrawled, For Sale-Call *** ****. I hate the siding, the interior is not cozy, turns out the main floor is one apartment and the upper storey is two small ones. We buy it. We're the Constantineaus of Evans Road.

the list of things
we think we need
shorter now

Celebrating My Fiftieth Birthday

I open wine and set it in the breathing space between us. A birthday that lasts a day, then fifty years of that day. The gift is always small, say, a beach stone found last year.

no price
too steep
to climb

WE ARE ALL ADULTS HERE

No denying our greying hair, the wrinkles on our cheeks. I face my grown nephews, of sorts, and see them for the men they are. Their partners hover nearby, the children of one also nearby, the newly acquired son-in-law close too. There are not so many years between me and them, Still, my age and my placement on the family tree is acknowledged. We value each other more now than in our younger iteration. All these headstones have given weight to the loss of parents, grandparents, siblings, other aunts and uncles, all of this, all of this loss, has given weight to we who are left, and to our mortality.

my brother's smile
on my nephew's face
all that's left to me

I Blame The Last Drink

Rosie waited so long for me to come home that she was peeved and primed. The second I opened the door she was gone. I ran out behind her but she was rounding the corner before I was within earshot. I watched her round the second corner and prayed I'd catch up. Not even close, corner after that, I saw everything. Three days away from the fix, the silly bitch found a long-haired shaggy guy who was willing and able. The rest is history. Now there's an unplanned pregnancy to be dealt with and of course the father's nowhere to be found.

the increase
in the moon
incremental

YOU

I was green back in the day, believed in love and empathising. Then you came along. Now I know, there are some roots you shouldn't put down. So many seeds that ought to be left unsown. And yes, places not gone.

In the heat of a wondrous day, bed messed, heart sore, I came to my senses. But when I finally rolled away, all I was, was gone.

all the things
we never said
stone in my shoe

Yearning

Playing that video game again—the one where the avatar, who works at the male strip club, looks like the neighbor's husband. Imagining. Projecting. Hoping.

crescent moon
rises on Valentine's Day
flat screen romance

Fifteen And Counting

End of the driveway, her stepdad, cell phone in one hand, pleading in the outstretched palm of the other. Somewhere enroute, on the other end of that cellphone connection, her father. Truths not told; realities not checked; hearts broken; a mom shattered; a sister in panic.

backpack in one hand
teddy bear in the other
striking out

Let Spring Be Spring

First-day, first-day a chant I repeat to myself in the quiet of early morning. The silence broken by the click of the switch on the coffee maker, the hiss of steam, and the weighty plop of water-now coffee filling the carafe. The kitchen fills with the fragrance of dark roast. I slide my favourite mug across granite.

I turn the page on the calendar to April. I utter a hope, a prayer, don't be cruel April, be true. Don't fool with us today, let spring be spring.

edge of the road
the stink of dog poop
snow melt

Before This Gathering And God Uttering The First Lie Of Her Marriage

This virtual wedding with its covid altered romance of the times is charming. Attendance is limited. The chosen ones are true friends and close family. The bride begins her vows at the same time as her tears. She turns to the assembled and declares, "I never cry,"

handfasting
the bride knotted up
inside

Truths

I listen to his persuasive deep voice. The cadence, the confidence, allows him to raise and lower hope as I follow along, already anticipating the punch line. The honest truth, he says. The *honest truth* like there's a dishonest truth available.

adult
adulation
adultery

Reclaimed

Blame still bubbles in me. A sour cherry phantom popped into my mouth, my face a puckered mass. His fault? Should blame be split between two? I hear the grind and squeal of brakes on a passing bus and force my jaw to relax. He's been gone a while, but I can still smell his aftershave.

dusk refilling the drawer with my things

I Change My Clothes

Feeling spiff in the powder blue top with the coordinating pants.
My husband walks into the room, exclaims, "There's my little
Smurfette!"

Louboutin heels
the height of fashion
not for the weak

Ho Ho Ho Boomed Out From Behind

I want to be like my mother. She slips her nylon stockings on each morning and rolls the excess above her knee in a garter. Sometimes a piece of underwear elastic, sometimes a rubber ring from a canning lid. I'm fascinated by the mark on her leg at night when she reverses the process.

The girls' group at the church is having a special service and I wear my uniform skirt and blouse, tie on the special ribbon tie. I'm ten and I've spent my weekly allowance on a pair of nylon stockings. I slip them over my feet and up my skinny legs, enjoying the feel. I've found a couple of broken rubber rings and when I've pulled the stockings up high enough that they don't show under the edge of my skirt I tie a ring at the top of each one.

Walking up the steep hill toward home after church I notice the old guy who plays Santa Claus every year coming along behind me. He's been to church too. I'm close to the top of the hill, so I speed up my step, flexing what passes for thigh muscle. That's when it happens. The knot in a rubber ring lets go. One stocking pools at my ankle. I have a choice, slip off my shoe and remove the stocking or fix the knot. But then, the Santa guy.

the biggest drawer
filled with silken things
adult addiction

A Coconut

I'm perched on the crossbar of his shiny red pedal bike, caged by his muscular arms. I've hitched a ride to my grandma's house that's up the street from his place. Up to now, I've trusted him. My mom lets him in the house, plus, he plays Santa Claus every year. A hundred kids, me included, have climbed up on his generous lap. We're passing his place when he asks the question. "You ever had fresh coconut?" "No," I say.

He stays on the bike seat and wheels us right to the front door of his one room shack. Pushing the door open wide, he bikes us into the cool dim interior. I don't know whether to jump and run or stay put, I've been fooled and fondled before by others. The place is tidy. The bed is made, his clothes are hung on nails along the walls, and there's a small collection of books.

Dead center on the table is a real coconut split into pieces. Its white flesh seems to glow in the light coming in the small window. He reaches for two chunks and shows me how to bite into it. The taste is unlike anything I've ever had. When we're finished, he takes the bit of shell from me and tosses the refuse into a rusty trash barrel. He backs the bicycle out into the sunlight.

a life built
on shaky knees
giving my all

VANITY

It's not like I travel with a compact mirror admiring my own special features. Yes, my eyes are the delphinium blue of my mother's and I like that. Yes, I inherited the same small space between my straight front teeth that my mother had, I like that. If I were to dye my hair, I might choose dark walnut, but I don't since my hair is now the same silver of my grandmother's locks. Is that vanity, or is that gratitude? This, however, I am choosing to be vain about. In my circle several of my friends are wearing my hair style. The style I adopted when I was thirty-eight and never changed. I think they admire mine and that says in this small way, they admire me. I like that.

small changes
this secret sauce
all mine

For Now

Wearing the T-shirt of choice for the day, I sink into the box of the short-ride wheelchair. Results day, both yearned for and dreaded. The doctor smiles—still not trusting. I tug at the hem of my shirt and wait for words because I already know smiles can fake you out. Then he says, we're releasing you from care. No more hospital parking lot traffic jams, no more bad choice deli smoked meat on rye in a cafeteria filled with patients, and doctors. I'm free.

free radicals
more than one way
to celebrate

He Doesn't Get The Joke

I hand the cell phone to him, ask him to read a narrative poem that's caught my attention, tickled my sense of the ridiculous, made me shake my head at the familiar reality played out on the screen. I stir my scrambled eggs and fork up a bite, waiting for the moment he gets to the punchline, waiting for the smile of shared amusement he will send across the steaming coffee cups between us, and   nothing

across the lake
a loon's laughter
echoes

SCHEDULES

The trickledown of routine—rule following is deep in me. For my mother, each day had a purpose, sometimes known to me, sometimes not. One thing for sure, Friday was shopping downtown day and Saturday was visit grandma. We ate supper at five o'clock on the dot, no wavering. If you were not there when the food hit the table, it was either cold or gone.

simple things
set in a kaleidoscope
then comes rain

For years I had dinner ready to be served when my husband got home from work. Five-thirty sharp. Then there was a reorganization of schedules where he was employed. He began his day earlier, came home earlier, five o'clock. He asked that suppertime stay the same. Try as I might, I couldn't do it. The minute his hand touched the doorknob, dinner was served.

structure
the key to control
inside me

BACK TO THE WALL

Blue, been dirt-dog, been yellow. Been back to the wall, lonely, broke and survived. Can't mistake a rose for a thorn, but tough and strong shows through the cloud on any day. I'll be around when the rose is gone, back to the wall, strong.

sidewalk crack
a small tuft of green
the long way home

Passages

I no longer fear my mother will arrive unannounced in one of her cache of stylish dresses. Her romance-novel heroine's hair fluffed out so it is barely contained by a hat of high style. She can't come back from the dead, that I'm sure of.

Still, old habits. I take the time to run a cotton swab along each ridge of the appliances in my kitchen, knowing she will still judge my housekeeping if the afterlife allows glimpses of the now. She thought me careless. Time after time, after time, she attempted to change my mind, guy after guy, this guy.

Marriage is so *permanent*, she said. Can't you *live* together, she said. A moving van is *cheaper* than a divorce, she said. My heart, his heart was, and remains, steadfast. That pulsing organ, where pith has stored every memory from first kiss to last fight, this heart's constancy sustains me and him. He loves me more now, than then, he says.

I study the enamelled sink. A hundred years of dishes washed in this farm house. Rust has eaten away the edge of the faucet's base as time has eaten away at my imagined inadequacies. Babies were bathed here, and soon, our grandchild will splash in this pseudo tub.

This daughter will remember days of judge and be judged. But a living goddess, who loves with abandon, who bathes babies splashing with joy, we will have no fear. We are strengthened by passages of time, after time, after time.

my breasts
ignore the summons
night nursing

GOT HER SIX

She'd lie on the old daybed in what served as a communal living room and dining room way before the term open concept was anyone's architectural dream. She'd place a basin beside her on the floor, just in case. This was always on a Sunday morning, when the Saturday party raged on beyond her tolerance. A day later everything would be back to normal, for six days.

high kites
love of whiskey and water
not so secret

PRISTINE

Twitter-fest of post winter storm tweets. A kid photographed mid-leap into side-of-the-path snow and the flashback is instantaneous. New snow unmarked by man or beast. I jump on my toboggan and push off down the steep incline from road to back yard of some stranger. Half down I hit an unseen obstruction hard enough to crumple the front of my aluminum toboggan, crunching my shins on the wooden rope bar. I hope this kid's head doesn't find a rock in that pristine snow.

unknown delight
behind every cool facade
potential

PINK

He says hey, want to see my rabbit? I'm five, I like rabbits. He leads me out to the back porch, where he stops, unzips, shows me his penis. I'm no fool, I have brothers, rabbits have fur and ears. I run like I was told to do.

porch light
the only witness
to his lie

Say Uncle

He likes pie. He likes an evening walk. His one talent is his ability to move his entire scalp by lifting his bushy eyebrows just so. His short, black hair gliding forward and back over his skull a mystery I've never solved. Mostly he is a wastrel. Yes, he likes pie. Yes, he likes an evening walk. Yes, he likes a peep through the upstairs bedroom keyhole.

bending the light
gnarled hands clutch
the old bible

Sadness

never going to bump into him at the big box, or the grocery store, or car shows, or the medical office. It's too late to come clean, to explain the reasons for the missing months.

omission
what we become
with time

Many Times

I've wanted to call and say things like, I've learned how not to kill a Christmas cactus and I can prove it. The one on my living room side table is over a year old and still healthy. Or, like today, I would have said I finally have an answer to that question from fifteen years ago about breaking up ground beef in spaghetti sauce, so it's fine, the way it is in the canned sauce. That I know how to grow and process my own tomatoes. I've wanted to call and say that.

weighted blanket
finally aware
of what was lost

NEVER RESTED

She said his penis was like a directional finder with a solar panel,
never off. Girl after girl after girl bearing his children. She must
have felt the sting, but she never chastised him—she bore eleven
of her own, she did.

sunny spot
between two wives
finally at rest

To The Last Drop

This birthday gift, a colourful coffee mug, reminds me of him. It becomes a shadowed moment on a sunny day. With its appliqued pictures of the Fab Four, he's even managed to ruin my nostalgia for *Sgt. Pepper's Lonely Hearts Club Band* album.

The best gift he ever gave me, was his goodbye.

recycle pickup
a second goodbye
to the Beatles

Happy Hours

On the untrimmed grass below the kitchen window a baby bunny is chewing the tops of mauve clover blossom. A robin flies into the scene, to land nearby. At first, they eye each other cautiously. Then the bunny takes two hops toward the robin. In response, the robin hops twice away. The bunny goes back to the clover and the robin hops closer, then closer and closer still to nab a worm. The bunny's head rises and its ears twitch. The next few minutes I watch a tableau of play between the two. Without warning a crow's caw from the pine. The bunny runs, the robin sounds a warning and flees. The crow caws again.

bar flies
over appetizers
office workers mingle

Thinking Through

Breathe, breathe in. Take note of the blossom in the air, the newly mowed grass. Listen to the sounds of birds and bees about their deeds. Birds build nests to raise their young. Bees will draw pollen from every flower, making sustenance for some and sweetness for others. At dusk, wait for the arrival of moon and stars. A pearl. Diamonds.

mother's fancy
tales readied for visitors
who never visit

FINAL FLIGHT

In Canada, when you live in the middle, doubtless your sister will choose to live on the edge. Vancouver is a full three provinces away with each province bigger than the size of some small countries. Beloved niece, born ten days before my own birthday, becomes a favorite. My fragile health makes me think this visit will be my last. The time with her is filled with love and weighted with sadness. On the flight home, alone and grieving, certain I will never fly again, I cry and cry and cry. I cry so much the man next to me pays for my wine.

craving hugs
the phantom pain
of lost parts

Home

Arborist was lettered on the truck's door, a truck that rocked loudly to a stop on the street. A short man jumped down from the driver's seat and walked a circle around the tall cedar tree in the neighbour's front yard.

A younger man stepped onto the sidewalk, then moved to the truck's rear. Chain saws and rope came out. In no time the top of the tree was lassoed, pulled taut toward the ground by the assistant. The loud wail of the chain saw filled the sunny day until the trunk was laid bare and released from the rope. A woodchipper, unseen, but heard now from its position in the back of the truck, chewed the branches to nothing. When the trunk is finally cut what's left of the tree falls to the lawn with a muffled thud and bounce.

Less than fifteen minutes and they'd felled and chewed the cedar to a pile of chips. Any evidence of their presence they swept up and the arborist and his man drove off.

For days I'd watched a nesting pair flit in and out of that tall bushy cedar. I'd eavesdropped on their courtship trills. I'd witnessed their scavenging trips for string and twigs. This morning they'd gone off, possibly to fill themselves after their hard work, or maybe one more twig was needed.

new development
each house the same
but different

BITS OF FANCY

She'd prep our cups, generously adding milk. Pour the tea, choosing the pouring height of the fragrant stream to maximize results. She'd say, "My, look at all those bubbles, sup them up, you'll be rich." I'd giggle, as she intended.

end of a sun shower
mother to child to child
old wives' dreams

GOOD FENCES

When he spotted me, he did a one-eighty, and headed back where he'd come from. Not only that, his face was red, flushed like someone caught doing something they shouldn't. I caught up and said hello. He replied, but he was twitchy. So twitchy it was beyond obvious. I said what are you doing in my neck of the woods? He said, "I was just going to check on something at the uh, you know, drug store." That was weird because he lived in the next small town over with its own drug store. Later on, I mentioned to his wife that I'd seen him in town on the street, and he was acting weird. She laughed, said he'd been playing around and she'd caught him. Said she'd given him the ultimatum, and when I saw him, he was on his way to close a rental mailbox where his side piece would send him love letters. I said "Who writes love letters anymore?" She said, "Who keeps them? Bastard doesn't know it yet, but he's going to be broker than broke when I'm through with him."

loose dog
a hole in the fence
greener pastures

I Know What I Said But

It's not the chaps that ride low on lean hips not that dancer's walk light and tall and confident like the pole is a living breathing thing that can be grabbed onto at any second not the way a moment turns into an hour while the recycling bins are lugged out to the curb not the bursts of easy laughter not blue eyes not the look back from blue eyes

night fire
his heart the hottest
my truth

Hard Times Good Times

Icicles grow long on a corner eave. Not quite pointed, thrusting by its nature, heedlessly breaking invisible seams, and slowly settling into its dripping finish.

kissed
by the sun and it's done
last cigarette

The Price Of Adult Humour

His mother and his wife dance around the kitchen preparing the evening meal. I'm a fixture in their house, my sister and the girl who lives here are best friends.

He's at the end of the table, a cigarette going to ash between his stained fingers. He winks at me and I step closer. He's fun, kind. His thin legs are crossed at the knee. He's in a semi slump, not sober, but not all the way gone either. He grins, asks a previously unheard question, "Are you your daddy's little squirt?"

Behind me his wife chokes on a half laugh, half gasp and says his name. I know there's a joke at my expense, but at my age I don't know the cost. His mother says, "That's enough" But he's feeling feisty and repeats the question. I say, "My dad's dead." He says "Well, he wasn't always."

the snap
of clean sheets
on the line

Rural Rides

On this summer evening we are doing what we love, taking a slow ride down a long narrow dirt road near our camp. To one side of the dirt track in a wide field we spot a farmer on a green John Deere busily baling hay in the last hours of the lowering sun. The sweet smell of the cut fills our nostrils. We pull off to watch. The farmer makes a gathering run that brings him close to where we are parked. He stops and we can see the concentration on his suntanned face as he flips a long lever and looks to the rear of his machine, pausing a second to note our presence.

The round cover rises and tightens and we hear the whirring as the machine does its binding work. A minute later the cover rises and a large round bale rolls off a short ramp to thud onto the ground. The farmer is watching us as we watch the process, and when it is done, we laugh and applaud out the open van window. He rises from his seat, doffs his cap and bows low, showing us the pink and shiny top of his bald head. He rises and laughs, as good as an actor in a play, before settling in to continue his task. We drive away.

real life
no screens no icons
no role playing

Fruit Of the Plum

Ten years after buying our house and turning it into a home, the gnarly tree we'd argued over—one of us wanting to chop it down the other to leave it—began to change.

warm days
shedding winter coats
snake's skin on the grass

Nothing about the trunk was different; the tree's bark still sprung out in spots, hanging like loose scales on a fantasy dragon. What we noted were the small bulging spots proliferating on each spindly branch. Being unseasoned gardeners and landscape ignoramuses, we passed it off as either leaf growth or pending death and went about ignoring it again.

June bride
straightening her vintage veil
a clutch of buds

One day we stepped outside and stopped, stunned by the magical overnight appearance of white blossom covering the entire tree. The thin trunk seemed almost a string tied to a cloud. Soon the blossoms fell. Hard pea-shapes took their place and as spring moved to summer, summer moved to fall, we watched plums form, grow, ripen and fall to the ground.

twenty years
of birds' drunken reveling
fermented plums

Single Focus

My husband is watching a video of a car repair in progress. Six failed attempts to set the engine in time results in engine revving in the way only an old, out of tune engine can. The narrator announces there will be a seventh attempt. I give my husband the look. The one that clearly says, really? Again? His response is a look of surprise followed by the apparent realization that I am not enjoying the repeated cacophony. In the time it has taken us to have this silent interaction, the engine has once again revved and the narrator has proclaimed it fixed.

afternoon ride
my mindless humming
earns the look

I Sit Quietly Waiting for Breakfast

A low utterance announces his displeasure. He's unable to wait for a pancake to form a golden crust, for the indicator bubbles to begin to pop. Delia Smith, British chef and PBS star, had taught me this and more. Back when I was hungover and only capable of lying in and dreaming of food prepared precisely, painstakingly, she was the go-to. That word again as he rinses another streak of runny batter off the spatula.

Sunday brunch
profanity pancakes
a house specialty

Time Change

And just like that, the arrival of the sun is moved ahead. The first glow, a patch of light on the living room floor, is pushed away. Meals times are unreliable, hunger is confused. Oatmeal and coffee, sandwich quarters, dinner plates and fruit pies are shuffled to appeal. Everything is on hold for an hour.

no head
for business schedules
city chickens

The Forgotten One

I don't think of him every day. Suicide is a cold river. When his face comes into my mind, or I come upon a memento I've kept , I pause without intending to pause. Today it's a letter with a poem on the back of the lined notebook page. The decision to hand off this ink and soul to his brother and his wife and the niece and nephew who love him is an easy one.

It's theirs to hold.

the child of the sixties
man of the nineties
winsome words

LET'S SEE WHAT YOUR HAIR WANTS TO DO

That's a new line on me. The cape is the same black plastic, the tissue neck guard is the same around my throat, hands have run through my hair a number of times. Now she's contemplating my reflection in the tall mirror. My regular stylist became a grandma and quit her job on the spot, new stylist, different approach. I'm spun, tipped, sprayed, shampooed, conditioned, and combed. She doesn't want to hear what I want. She wants to do what my hair wants. Soon I'm clipped, blown dry, fifty bucks poorer, with a hairstyle popular with ladies of a certain age.

hanging out
in the noonday sun
new crop

Where We Differ

I knock, then enter the bedroom where the grandmother of the bride is dressing for the wedding. She's on her way to being the Gramma at the wedding with the best undergarments in which she is now clad.

The scent of talc *Lavender by Yardley* is familiar to me. A light dusting as always, patted on after her bath. As a child I would watch a cloud rise and disperse, the mauve of the powder puff moving across her bosom. All through my teens, I waited to be similarly endowed. It became obvious with time I'd not inherited my mom's figure.

Today, I look at her pink cheeks, her bright blue eyes, and her still-brown hair pinned high atop her crown in the style she loves. She is who she has always been. I move to stand behind her and do something I've wanted to do for years—I tighten the straps of her bra, moving the adjuster up a good four inches.

In the mirror she watches her cleavage reappear, cheeks flush even pinker, and she says, "Hey, hey, my girl, I'm not out to catch a man."

war time
all the reasons to marry
changed now—#metoo

CONTINUITY

It's the fortieth anniversary of my marriage to my husband, and his to me, on Sunday. He has something on the calendar, so here we are on Saturday having an early dinner at one of our favorite restaurants. I've brought out my cell phone and set it on the table. I'm not a chronic phone checker, we talked about this beforehand, my husband and I. There's no rush, we order drinks and when they arrive, I tell the server it's our anniversary celebration. I have my phone ready and ask if she will snap a photo. She says sure and how many years is it? We tell her and she's loud in her exclamation, she says she'll have been married half that time later in the month. She takes several pictures and hands back my phone.

As always, the food is delicious and obviously the company is comfortable after all these years. We have no plan to eat dessert, we discuss the tip and prepare to pay the bill. The restaurant this early in the afternoon is not crowded, there's one young couple and a grandma with her granddaughter. The server comes to the table, leans in and says "your bill has been taken care of." Well! We're surprised and ask how that happened and she tells us the young couple is 'paying it forward' and wish us a happy anniversary. It's their fifteenth anniversary next month.

On our first anniversary, different restaurant, we were enjoying each other's company and one of the customers of the shop where my husband works stops at our table. He greets my husband who introduces us and mentions our anniversary. The man wishes us a happy anniversary just as our food arrives and he leaves the restaurant. We eat together and agree to skip dessert. The server comes to clear away the dishes and says, "Your cheque is taken care of, paid by the gentleman who was speaking with you earlier."

special events
recur and return
as gifts

As An Older Person

I gave up robes when I moved to voluminous floor length granny gowns of heavy cotton flannel. My last robe was a cheap one, faded blue, unidentified fiber, bought for a hospital stay. It was too long, which I fixed by cutting it to ankle length and didn't even bother hemming.

When I was young my robes were useless monstrosities like the one my daughter has on today, a champagne beige, bottom skimmer, unbelted with more collar than length.

Once, on Christmas, my mother surprised me. She sat on the sofa grinning like a Cheshire cat as I ripped giftwrap revealing an extremely *un*revealing wide-leg flannel jumpsuit complete with matching flannel robe which I admit, I grew into wearing. I'd walk down the hall and laugh at a shadow resembling Darth Vader's cape as he stalked on the bridge of the death star. Physically, I'm more Yoda than Darth. Like all jumpsuits it was hell going for a pee. The movie score is the latest earworm.

sexy is in
the beholder's eye
cataract blurred

Predictions

I'm in my early teens. Our habit of reading our letters aloud prevails. Today Mom is reading a letter from my sister-in-law. She's written to say they won't be over for their usual visit; my brother is booked for a vasectomy on the Friday, nobody knows if he'll be travel-worthy.

Mom, a wife whose husband roamed free in a garden of Lilies, Violets, Roses, and Irises gave her usual opinion of undesirable news. "Huh! Everybody knows, you fix a dog and all they're good for is laying on the porch getting fat."

Mother's Day
on his back on the grass
taunting a vulture

Freedom

I am a child and blissfully unaware of the gift of freedom I've been given. My mother, after shepherding all ten of my brothers and sisters, is obviously tired. As long as I am within shouting distance, she is content to let me be me. Me being me is another gift I am unaware of. The two gifts are the making of my creativity. As I run wild, so does my imagination. I am a television chef, a singer, a lonely person, a happy person, and a loved person. I learn to think in the spaces of silence.

under the eyes of helicopter parents will there be poets

New Dollar Store Plant Pots

The garden was my mother's oasis. She'd rise with the summer sun, hum as she pulled a thin cotton dress over her slip and disappear daily to weed. I would move to the vacated spot in the bed and lie content in her residual body heat to doze off again.

Years later, through growing pains and mother/daughter relationship faltering, I am invited to lunch at my daughter's. Ushered into a tiny living room, my breath catches. A green-thumb oasis fills containers and corners and for a moment I am the child in my mother's garden.

pot
another word
for happy

Acknowledgements

I am filled with gratitude for my late mother, Grace, and my sister, Marie. The friendship and mentorship of Irene Golas has been invaluable; the fellowship of Haiku Canada members and the Haiku Society of America motivating; Thomas Leduc, Betty Guenette, MaryAnne Boulet, for the reasons you know. I value the many journals that teach through reading.

I appreciate the guidance of Heather Campbell of Latitude 46 Publishing and the care and expertise of Denise Fontaine-Pincince, editor of this collection.

A number of these pieces previously appeared, in one form or another, in the following: The Haibun Journal, Modern Haiku, Failed Haiku, Presence Haiku Journal, The Wales Haiku Journal, bottlerockets, Northern Exposure, a haibun anthology by members of Haiku Canada, and three lines at a time.

About the Author

Vera Constantineau's poetic focus is in Japanese forms, haibun, haiku, senryu and tanka. In addition to poetry, her non-fiction essay, Options, is included in Against Death—35 Essays on Living (Anvil Press, 2021). In 2021 her haiku placed third in the Martin Lucas Haiku Award "Presence Haiku Journal" in Britain, her essay He and I placed third in the 2021 Northwestern Ontario Writers Workshop Creative Non-fiction prize and in 2014, she was awarded first place in the Bangor Maine Haiku Society annual prize. Her short fiction and haiku have appeared in journals around the world including; Canada, Japan, USA, UK, India and Europe. She is a member of the Sudbury Writers Guild, Haiku Canada, Haiku Society of America, and Tanka Canada. She served as the sixth poet laureate for the City of Greater Sudbury (2020-2022). She lives in Sudbury with her husband.